RESTAURANT
BUSINESS

HOW TO START AND BE SUCCESSFUL

ANTHONY EKANEM

Contents

Preface

Having your own restaurant business is one of the most fulfilling and enjoyable business ventures. Food is a renewable commodity. This means people would not stop looking for food because eating out is both entertaining and functional.

Many people dream of doing a restaurant business, whether it is fast food, coffee shop or gourmet. Many people fail to sustain their operation, and most of them go out of business in their first year of business. This is a result of lack of preparation and dedication by the owner. Many people jump into the restaurant industry too fast without weighing the pros and cons of the project or having the necessary knowledge and expertise.

However, there is a way to reduce the risk that is associated with new ventures such as restaurant businesses. Preventive planning and proper management are the keys to success, but there are also minor things that count in the whole process of owning a restaurant.

Every business needs a business plan to succeed. Business plans lay down the different conditions and characteristics that should be integral in the business. The availability of a carefully formulated business plan is a step towards success. You will find details about creating a business plan in a later chapter; however, some points to consider are:

1. **Description of the Restaurant's Concept**

The objective and the general concept of the restaurant must be specified. This will give an overview of what the restaurant intends to do and for whom it plans to do it. The concept of the restaurant must be established because it is the core idea by which everything else will depend.

There are many things to consider in designing the overall concept of the restaurant, such as:

a. The type of restaurant you intend to run
b. The unique features it would have which would set it apart from similar restaurants in the locality
c. The overall selling factor of the restaurant

2. **The Target Market**

The target market of the restaurant must be identified. No restaurant should target all kinds of people. Even fast-food restaurants have a specific target market, even though it may seem at first that it caters to people of all classes.

The concept of the restaurant must be aligned with the target market. The target market would depend on the owner of the restaurant, and the selection can be based on the type of food or the personal preference of the owner.

3. **Food Category, Food Items and Prices**

Before starting your restaurant business or even before you entertain the thought of opening a restaurant, the kind of food to be served must be identified first. Most restaurant owners put up their restaurants according to their favourite kind of food. Some restaurants are inspired by one-time experiences such as eating delicious foreign foods.

Many choices are available for aspiring restaurant owners. The food categories should be identified next. The exact items on the menu should also be identified. The pricing of these items is critical because it will determine the feasibility of the business.

4. Financial Evaluation

After you have determined the prices of the food items have, it is time to develop the financials of the project. You can employ a professional consultant to assess the financial sustainability of the restaurant. Every project costs and risks should be stated in the business plan.

5. Ownership

An enthusiastic entrepreneur may consider creating a small corporation or a partnership or a sole proprietorship to give the restaurant a legal status. Check with your local authorities the requirements for establishing such a business.

6. Marketing Plan

Include a marketing plan because it is essential to the success of the restaurant.

You should consider other things before going into the restaurant business. What is listed above are only part of the whole scheme of a restaurant establishment. The restaurant must reflect your preferences to make it enjoyable to operate. However, a lot of consideration should be given to how it is going to generate money because this is the only way the restaurant will be sustainable.

We have covered some of the vital points about having a business plan for a restaurant. This subject and other relevant planning information are treated in-depth in subsequent chapters.

CHAPTER ONE

Types of Restaurants You Can Run

Businesspersons who are thinking about starting their own restaurant business should understand that restaurants are generally good business ventures. Why? Because people are always looking for food. And eating cannot stop.

There are different types of restaurants that business people can run, and the decision regarding what kind of restaurant or what style to put up depends on various factors. The decision regarding the general idea of a restaurant business will depend on different factors. Listed below are some of these factors:

1. **The Location**

The style of the restaurant will depend on the location. For instance, if you are thinking of establishing a Chinese-style restaurant in an area where there are many Chinese restaurants, you might want to tweak some details about your restaurant to have a competitive advantage. You may stick with the general concept of a Chinese restaurant because the place is famous for Chinese cuisine, but you may need to add some different kinds of cooking as well to give it a fusion.

2. The Target Market

The target market is crucial in determining the style of restaurant to set up. A busy environment where class B society booms may be an ideal location for a medium-sized fast-food restaurant. Different restaurants cater for different types of people, and no one restaurant type can capture the whole of the market because it would only end up in confusion.

3. Availability of Materials

An up-and-coming restaurant might want to look closely at the availability of the materials in the location of interest. For example, a seafood restaurant will depend largely on the availability of fresh ingredients and seafood in the local market. If not, you will have to look for alternatives which can cost you additional money.

4. Availability of Good Cooks

There are more than adequate restaurants in many places today. What separates the good ones from the average one is the quality of cooks they have. The style and layout of the restaurant should match the skills and experience of the chef. Some good chefs can easily adjust to styles which they are not familiar with, but they can be very hard to find, and perhaps, they will ask for big pay.

5. Personal Preference

Although every business is built on vision, the personal preference of the owner will ultimately determine the type and style of restaurant that will be set up. There are ways to beat the usual odds which go against the success of a new restaurant business.

There are different styles of restaurants from which you can choose. These are:

1. Steakhouses

These restaurant type usually cater to the middle and upper-class markets. These are also traditionally oriented towards families and have a very relaxed and homely atmosphere. The meals in steakhouses are generally believed to be good buys. There are also the high-end steakhouses which concentrate more on the quality of the meat they serve.

2. Seafood Restaurants

There are diverse types of seafood restaurants available. There are the quick-service ones, the ones that cater for the middle class and the higher-end ones which cater to the upper-class segment of the society. The quick-service seafood restaurants are very similar to fast-food restaurants. Usually, seafood restaurants offer a wide variety of seafood, and they serve it in different ways.

3. Casual Eating

This type of restaurant caters for all kinds of people irrespective of the social class. People go there so they can have many food choices and enjoy the relaxed atmosphere.

The prices in casual dining restaurants are generally not that high.

4. Pizzeria

There are two options in creating a pizzeria. The first one is to construct a complete restaurant which does not only serve pizzas but many kinds of food as well. The other choice is to specialise in pizzas and a few other items such as soft drinks and ice-cream.

5. Coffeehouse

More and more people are now going to coffeehouses. These coffeehouses offer very cosy atmospheres for small talks and coffee conversations.

Above are only a few of the options you have when it comes to developing a concept for your restaurant business. Feel free to explore other options and stick with the one that satisfies you most.

CHAPTER TWO

Designing Your Restaurant

Good design and layout plans are necessary for a good restaurant. A restaurant is a business than can be very fulfilling. The mere fact that people come to your restaurant to eat is already something to value. It is like having people in your home now and then, longing for your home-baked goodies.

A successful restaurant plan will have a good design and layout. Design and layout plans depend on different factors which will influence the final decisions later. The output of the layout plans can affect the success of the restaurant. These are little things that can influence the customers to go to another restaurant calling out to their taste buds.

After identifying the type of food and services, the next step is to hire consultants to handle the design of the restaurant. These are the things you must consider when deciding the design and layout plans for your restaurant.

1. **Density of customers**

The layout plan should target mostly the comfort of the customers. Even fast-food restaurants consider the density of people, especially during peak hours, although these restaurants become too crowded during lunchtime.

For formal eating restaurants which cater to the upper-class, it may be wise to provide more space between the tables since these restaurants do not rely on many people per day. Their revenues depend on the pricing of their food and not on the number of customers. There should be adequate provision for eye candy such as furniture and artworks.

2. Style of service

The general layout and floor plans of the restaurant should also be based on the type of service that the restaurant will provide. Fast-food restaurants and self-service restaurants would require less distance between the tables since the food will not be served there. For other restaurants that offer table service, the spaces between the tables are important to prevent too clutter from happening in a part of the restaurant.

3. Type of building

The layout plan is limited by the type of structure where the restaurant will be built. You should consider all the different curves and the minor details in the structure before proceeding.

4. Lighting

Proper lighting is critical. The lighting should match the mood and type of food service rendered at the restaurant. A calm atmosphere can be complemented by bright lights, while subtler shades can accompany serene and serious moods.

Designing the restaurant is divided into two main parts: the dining and the production areas.

The dining area is important because it is the whole essence of the structure of the restaurant. The people should be comfortable eating in your restaurant, and this would be determined at the designing phase. Studies have shown that 50 per cent of the time, people go to restaurants in pairs; 30 per cent come alone while the remaining 20 per cent come in groups.

The production area is the second important part of a restaurant. The major consideration for the production area should be efficiency. The arrangement of the kitchen will determine the speed with which the food can be cooked and served. The production area design should take into contemplation other things like spaces for storage, food preparation, baking, cooking, waste storage, production aisles, employee facilities and such other matters.

In hiring design consultants, remember to insert a Confidentiality Clause in the contract. This is aimed at preventing the consultants from leaking any parts of the design to other people, especially to your competitors. This can be as simple as a single-sentence clause which states that you will own everything regarding the design.

The above are some important things you should remember when designing your restaurant. The most important thing to remember, of all, is the people that will be eating at the restaurant. The success or failure of your restaurant business depends on them.

CHAPTER THREE

Your Start-up Costs

The cost of starting your own restaurant business is one fundamental matter to be dealt with and often the most difficult to determine because, to a large extent, it depends on the type of restaurant that you wish to open.

Your restaurant start-up costs are drawn as expenses incurred for the procurement or creation of your restaurant business. Start-up costs include any incurred amounts or out-going capital relating to your restaurant's activity directed for income generation before your restaurant business starts.

Start-up costs typically include the following expenses:

- Potential markets surveys.
- Evaluation of supplies, labour and facilities
- Advertisements.
- Business equipment and fixtures
- Equipment and fixture installation
- Interior Decoration
- Employee uniforms
- Salaries for employees undergoing training
- Training costs
- Costs of travels for obtaining supplies
- Consultants Fees and other similar services

ESTIMATING YOUR START-UP COSTS

It is wise to study your start-up cost estimates with a competent accountant. Begin by recording and adding up your entire restaurant's equipment that you consider necessary to start and manage your new restaurant. Check out the chapter on selecting equipment and furnishings for more on this subject.

a. On your list, mark off items or equipment that are not necessary and can wait.

b. Decide what kind of equipment you need to buy brand new, and what type you can buy used.

c. Decide on the things you can lease for the moment.

d. When adding up the building or office cost of your restaurant, also remember to include the re-modelling costs, decoration costs, fixtures and fittings, installation and delivery fees for equipment.

e. Include professional fees, utility payments, permits and licenses.

f. When calculating your advertising costs, make sure you add trademarks, logo expenses as well as other graphics to be used.

g. Come up with ways you may lower some expenses. Call vendors and suppliers and work out specific deals.

h. Estimate that all expenses will be higher than expected. It is practical to add about 1-5 per cent to your estimate.

Write your business plan before you arrive at your final estimate for your start-up costs. Usually, a business plan functions to reveal more start-up costs that were not thought of. Again, refer to the chapter on preparing your business plan for a detailed discussion on this.

Include your restaurant's first three months to six months of operating investment in your start-up costs. These expenses usually include employee salaries, advertising costs, rent, supplies, delivery expenses, utilities, taxes, insurance premiums, maintenance, professional fees, loan payments, inventory, etc.

BEFORE OPENING YOUR RESTAURANT

You may want to work in, or volunteer in a similar restaurant like the one you intend to open. Doing this will enable you to understand menu development, restaurant marketing, payroll and many other elements of the food business.

1. **Determine your target market.** What type of market segment do you want to cater for? Is it teenagers, family or seniors? Determining your target customers before you start your business will help you organise your menu and establish your design, atmosphere and location of your business.

2. **Pick your food concept and style of service.** Typically, your service style can be fast-food, offering fries, burgers, sandwiches and hotdogs; mid-scale offering value-priced full course meals; or upscale, providing high-class ambience with full-service meals with higher prices.

3. **Develop a business plan.**Again, see the chapter on preparing a business plan but make sure your plan includes:

- Your restaurant's overall concept and objective
- Detailed financial projections
- Your menu and pricing
- Employee and equipment details
- Marketing and advertising plans

4. **Create your menu.**Understand that your menu can either make or mar your restaurant; therefore, it must conform to your restaurant's overall concept. We have devoted an entire chapter to menu creation.

5. **Choose your location.**Look for an area where there is a continuous flow of human and vehicular traffic, accessible parking space, and near or along with other businesses. The chapter on location will explain more.

6. **Know restaurant safety regulations.**Usually, restaurants are controlled and are subject to inspections by local authorities. You must know your local regulations and conform to them.

7. **Hire your employees.**Make sure that your employment announcements expressly declare your specific requirements.

Starting a new restaurant business comes with its challenges as well as rewards. Before starting any business, do your research first. Make sure you are right for entrepreneurship as well as recognise that significant effort is required. Therefore, it is important that you enjoy whatever you are venturing into and you must have confidence in your products or service because it will consume most of your valuable time, especially when you are just starting.

HOW TO ADVERTISE THE RESTAURANT

Positive public recognition is vital for your restaurant's success, and this recognition can be achieved through public relations campaigns and advertising.

Know that a public relations campaign and advertising are two different things. But both are meant to raise the interest of consumers in a service or product, and both generally use the same tools, like radio, television, print and the internet. Advertising uses ads, while public relations uses news.

Let us look at the major differences between advertising and public relations.

1. **Message control**

The how, where and when an advertisement flows, is quite controllable. An ad space bought in the right format like radio, broadcast, online, or print implies that you have control over the message that you want to disseminate.

On the other hand, while the message-creating process using public relations is also very controllable, what happens after your message has left, is usually uncontrollable; and this brings up the question of whether potential customers see the information you supplied as newsworthy. Public relations make sure this happens.

2. **Information Personalization**

Advertisement, being very expensive, does not provide enough room to customise or personalise your restaurant's story. A public relations campaign does this by creating stories from multiple angles aimed at successfully reaching various media channels like daily newspapers, business journals, food service publications, city magazines, entertainment and dining publications, national magazines, and so on. You can increase your broadcast and reach more audience that will be informed about your restaurant.

3. **Implied Endorsement**

In advertising, you pay someone to have your message filtered directly to your prospective consumers. Public relations, however, affords the reliability of an indirect endorsement of a third-party. This means you do not pay to get advertised, publications offered them to you free, giving you space to relay your restaurant's story to your prospective customers. An endorsement is an efficient tool in shaping public opinion.

4. **Cost-Effectiveness**

There is no comparison to the cost of display advertising in a magazine or publication to the cost of distributing and writing an enlightening press release. To hire a firm to create press releases for your restaurant is many times cheaper than advertising. Furthermore, press release articles reach more audiences since consumers are more interested in stories as opposed to advertisements.

5. **Life Span**

With public relations, a well-constructed story can capture the attention of the reader for a long time, where the viewer notices an ad in just about 5 minutes. Consumers usually clip some articles they read, such as a new holiday destination that they would like to visit or a new restaurant where they would want to sample their food.

Public relations aim to maintain a "noise" or sort of ongoing talks about your restaurant and what it offers and build credibility. There are many media houses that you can reach when you have made a "well-expressed" plan and the appropriate public relations company to execute it.

So, when will you start using public relations? Why and when should you advertise? The answers lie with you and you alone. It depends on your requirements and what you want to achieve. You can combine both advertising and public relations as your marketing tools, or separately as situations demand.

CHAPTER FOUR

Market Analysis

The food-service industry caters to the universal need of all humans – to be nourished. However, the way food appeals to humans is not universal. Humankind is a diverse group, and there is no single operation of food service that can satisfy this diversity. This is one reality that entrepreneurs in the restaurant business find challenging to accept. Many prospective entrepreneurs think they can catch everyone, but such efforts always end up in failure. They fail to realise that trying to cater to everyone results in not being able to cater to anyone at all.

It is better to concentrate on a small segment of the market. This way, you can offer the best services for that segment of your choice. This can be achieved by doing a market analysis – a study of the potential target market.

The "senior's market" is made up of people who are 65 years and older. Most seniors live on fixed incomes, from their pension or sustenance by relatives, and thus do not have flexible spending power. Most senior citizens usually go to family-oriented eating places such as lunch buffets because they offer good food and services at affordable prices. Less active seniors usually prefer smaller food portions as they may have a smaller appetite.

When targeting then seniors, it is good to make them special by offering seniors promotions or reduced rates. You can also market your restaurant as a senior-friendly restaurant by emphasising safety features such as ramps and handlebars.

The late adult market is made up of people aged 50 to 64 years old. They are usually the ones who experience empty nest syndrome, where grownup children have left home. This market segment usually has the most stable financial status as they could be in the most advanced stages in their careers. At this point, price usually does not matter. This is the age when many people just start to enjoy life and its pleasures fully. So, the main concern here is good food and excellent service. When targeting this market segment, it is good to present your restaurant with elegance and sophistication. It is wise to invest heavily in ambience and class.

The middle-aged group is made up of people who are around ages 40 to 50. These are very productive years because most executives and top career people fall under this market segment. Money is plentiful, and thus they spend with more generosity. In this age, the people are quite fond of trendy and high-end, fine-dining restaurants. Many people in this age bracket already have grandchildren, and this is also good for family-friendly eating places which are more formal than those frequented by the senior segment.

The young-adult market consists of people in their mid-twenties to those just before their middle age. This is an age of great effort for reputable families. The primary concern here is enjoying children and keeping a good relationship with them. People in this market segment usually look for eating places that are conducive for bonding with their children. It is important to provide comfort and a laid-back ambience for this market segment.

The young market comprises those in their early twenties and younger. This is probably the most diverse market segment. The main concern of the people in this market segment is instant gratification at low prices. This is the primary market for the fast-food industry. A good strategy for this market is to be updated with the latest trends and offering food services in addition to what is "cool" and "trendy".

CASH, CHECK OR CHARGE?

Probably, the most exciting part when establishing a restaurant, or any other business for that matter, is the collection of money. What is a business for, if not to earn money? For some people, the only concern is money. Money nowadays is no longer limited to a single monetary form but different modes as well, which may be called the three C's – cash, check, and card or charge. Which is the best mode to collect money? This could be a puzzling question for an aspiring entrepreneur. Hopefully, the following paragraphs will help explain things better.

1. **Cash: An Instant Gratification**

Possibly the most common form of money is cash. Nothing whets the appetite for a business like crisp new notes. It is the monetary form we are most familiar with, and the one most connected to profits and earnings. Cash is excellent because it is money in its simplest form – tangible and physical. It is instantly disposable and can be used anywhere.

However, more and more people try to avoid carrying cash these days. First, cash can be bulky to carry. Carrying a lot of money entails one to bring compacts of paper. Secondly, since cash is physical money, it is very risky and can be lost or stolen. Once it is gone, there is practically no way of getting it back. It can be easily stolen and can even lure danger by attracting robbers and other harmful elements. It may be dangerous to customers as they can easily be held up by criminals. It can impact the business negatively as well because it can easily be embezzled. While cash can give instant gratification, high security is needed to ensure its preservation.

2. Cheque: The Symbolic Cash

Cheques can be handy for people who have money in the bank. With cheques, you can still spend money without having to carry thick bundles of paper around. Cheques can be quite secure as the money it represents can only be claimed by the intended recipient, unless if the cheque is written paid to cash.

There are many advantages in using cheques, but there are also drawbacks that could inconvenience the recipient. Cheques need to be cashed, which takes time and extra effort for the collector. The money collected cannot be spent immediately. Cheques expire after a few months, usually after six months. Perhaps the greatest danger that cheques may entail is insufficient funds. The customer paying with a cheque may not have enough money in their account. It takes more time and efforts to gain the money earned.

3. Charge: A Promise to Be Redeemed

Plastic money (or credit card) is now a popular method of monetary exchange. It is very convenient and easy to use. It is easy to carry and has so much spending power. People love to use it because of the extra bonuses that come with it, such as airline miles and bonus gifts. On the recipient's end, money collection is sure, since the responsibility of payment rests on the credit card company, who bears the burden of pursuing criminal customers. The refunds may also be directly credited to the recipient's bank account, making the sale secure.

Convenient as it may be, credit cards are not devoid of disadvantages. Credit card companies typically charge substantial percentages of sales and could diminish your earnings. Money may also take time to collect, and there is more paperwork needed to claim the money. Credit card fraud is possible and can victimise both customers and restaurant owners.

Perhaps the best alternative of them all is the debit card. The debit card signifies everything good about cash with none of the drawbacks of cheques. A debit card purchase is like using real money. A debit card is like a credit card but works like a cheque or cash. When a customer presents their debit card, the merchant swipes the card the same way as a credit card. The chequing account of the presenter is inquired to determine if there are enough funds in the account to cover their purchase, and the amount is immediately deducted and transferred to the merchant's account. This is the next best option after cash!

FINAL WORDS

In deciding which method of payment is best for your restaurant business, the final choice depends on the customer. You should keep in mind what method is best for your customers to pay – what is most convenient for them with regards to their profile. It is not advisable for a place that caters to children and teens to accept only credit cards since most children would not have credit cards yet. It might not be advisable to refuse cheques or credit cards for fine dining that caters for executives, as prices could be high and bringing lots of cash could be very inconvenient and insecure. It is good to have all methods of payment available, so your customers can choose the one most suitable for them.

With a careful study of the benefits of each payment method, together with the market profile, you can choose the best payment option for your restaurant. Hopefully, the money will rake in by the bundles, whether in cash, cheque, or charge.

CHAPTER FIVE

How to Write Your Menu

Among the most consistent features in any decent restaurant is the menu. They are one of the very first things that greet you when you enter your favourite eating place as they are commonly posted at the entrance or immediately handed to you when you are seated. You read them, use them, and then forget them once the waiter has taken your order.

But menus do more than just listing what a restaurant offers. The menu is essential to the overall success of the restaurant. Everything in a restaurant's operation is connected to the menu, and that is why it is a critical matter to work on when running a restaurant. No matter how mundane the menu may seem to the layman, writing them correctly takes effort.

The writing of the menu does not start with the actual writing of what the restaurant can serve but begins way before that. The work of menu writing begins with the conception of the restaurant. At the inception of the restaurant, a theme should be set, and that theme should originate through all the rudiments of the eating place. Assortment doesn't work, while fusion may.

Whether it is Italian, Japanese, Continental Chinese, or modern, there should be a theme that will stand for the identity of the restaurant. The theme will govern what is inside the menu, from its first print throughout all future updates. Having the idea helps narrow down the menu, keeping it simple not only for the customers' eyes but also for the restaurant's inventory. The theme will tell you or the chef what to write and what not to include on the menu. At the same time, the theme will give the chef or cook an idea of what to include.

After establishing the theme of the restaurant and listing the likely items to include in the menu, the next thing is for the chef to write down the recipes of the menu items. While the recipes may not concern the menu, it is very connected to it as the operations in the kitchen are activated by the customers' orders, which are based on the menu.

The recipes will serve as important descriptions of what is on the menu. The recipes are vital to delivering the items on the menu as consistently as possible. If the chef cannot translate the recipe of an item simply enough for the cooks to replicate, then it is better to discard the item from the menu no matter how good it may seem. It is only after the recipes have been written can the menu be drafted.

After writing the recipe and drafting the menu, the next step is to contact suppliers that would provide the ingredients. The chef may be able to come up with recipes and a menu of delectable pieces, but they cannot be made and served if there are no ingredients. You and the chef should be able to source the items carefully and thoroughly. It is better to contact numerous suppliers to find one that can give the best quality, most consistent quantities, and most reasonable prices.

This stage in the menu writing also determines the prices of the food to serve. The costs of ingredients directly affect the selling price of the finished meals. At this juncture, it may be necessary for the cook to substitute some ingredients that may be too expensive, or in worse cases, discard a meal totally because the cost might make it difficult to serve at a reasonable price.

When you have made a good deal with suppliers, the next step is to test the menu. The chef must gather the menu and present it to the whole restaurant – the waiters, the managers, and everybody else involved in the service. This will acquaint the entire restaurant to the food and, at the same time, will help evaluate if the food will be good enough to serve or not. At this point, it is advisable to take pictures of the meals to serve as a guide for the staff so they will know how the finished meals would look like. After the tasting, the chef should know if there are changes to make in the menu, after which it can be finalised.

The last step will be the printing of the menus. Several menu suppliers will be able to present different types of menus and materials for the restaurant managers to choose from. You may select the booklet type of menu or a single-paged one. The options are endless. You may choose to outsource the printing of your menus, or you may opt to invest in a menu printer yourself should you deem it necessary to change the menu often the usual.

The menu may be a sheet of paper, or some sheets of paper, but it is an essential backbone of a successful restaurant. Writing a menu may be tedious, but the efforts to make one are worth it.

CHAPTER SIX

Furnishing Your Restaurant

Many people dream of setting up their restaurant and making it big on the food scene. However, most of these people stumble and fall because they do not know what it takes to have a decent dining place. A good restaurant theme, efficient staff, and reasonable prices are usually planned. However, one important thing may be overlooked, and that is acquiring equipment and furnishings. Here are some helpful suggestions for furnishing your restaurant.

When looking for restaurant equipment, the first thing you need to do is to research the type of equipment you need in your restaurant. The industrial kitchen is much more complicated than the one at home as meals are prepared several times more than just three meals a day. Building a restaurant kitchen is vital; you might consider hiring an expert for this, but if you do not have enough funds, you can still make it by carefully planning what to get.

Restaurant equipment and machines must be simple, doing just what they are expected to do. Those with unique features are often come with useless functions that are only included to increase their prices. Complicated machines can also result in complex malfunctions. What you need is an oven that bakes, broils, or roasts, not the one that tells you the time or rings when there is a burglary incident. It is also imprudent to buy equipment that has combined functions of usually different machines. If one of the functions becomes bad, it is more likely that the other functions will be affected in one way or the other, thus debilitating your kitchen two or three times more.

Acquiring restaurant equipment does not necessarily mean you have to buy it. You have the option to lease or rent equipment. Leasing is useful for those who do not have enough finances to purchase the equipment. Leasing also lets you pay for the machine or equipment only when it is needed to be used. The option of getting new equipment is more realistic with leasing. You can always get a replacement after the lease of the previous one expires.

Major maintenance of the equipment is the responsibility of the owner, which frees you of the costs of fixing broken equipment. The disadvantage of leasing is that it can be quite expensive in the long run. However, if you are earning a lot, then it might be worth it.

Some equipment that you can lease include coffeemakers, ice machines, dishwashers, and fabrics. Coffee-making machines can be acquired for free from companies that sell the coffee as long as you keep buying your beans from them. Ice machines can burn out quickly and is advisable to lease it to prevent the hassle of constant repairs. Dishwashers are quite expensive and leasing them may be an excellent solution to acquire them. And like coffee companies, some detergent manufacturers lend dishwashers to their loyal customers. Fabrics can also be leased, and usually, the lease includes laundering, delivery, and storage.

Some new equipment can be costly to buy. But you do not necessarily have to buy all equipment new. Many second-hand restaurant equipment stores can serve their purpose well as they cost far less than brand new ones. You must ensure there is an assurance from the seller that the equipment will work, at least for a reasonable period.

Dispensable pieces like knobs and nuts are acceptable not to be in perfect condition since you can replace them. What matters is the performance of the appliance. It should be able to work for a reasonable length of time when you can earn enough money at least to buy new equipment when the old one finally wears out. Among the equipment that is fine to purchase second-hand are gas ranges, fryers, ovens, grills, and tools such as tongs and mashers. They are simple equipment that lasts long enough for a second owner to use decently.

Acquiring equipment is one of the most important components of establishing a restaurant business. With meticulous planning, you can make the most out of your restaurant equipment, with the most affordable costs to you.

CHAPTER SEVEN

Hiring Your Staff

The food-service industry is one that involves a lot of personal relationships. Hiring excellent staff is one of the most crucial steps you can take when starting your restaurant. It could make or mar your restaurant, no matter how good the ambience, the facilities, or the location. The recruitment process in a restaurant could be very tedious, but fortunately, human resource practitioners have provided guidelines that can help you in hiring excellent restaurant staff.

The recruitment process for a restaurant does not start with the actual interview or with the posting of job advertisements. It begins with knowing what you want the staff to do. Having a general knowledge of what is required from the team will help you to create the job description, which is central for advertising the job vacancy and for shortlisting of applicants. The job description need not be too formal, but it must state in clear terms the responsibilities of the position. They should also list relevant credentials and skills that the applicants should have to be considered.

The next thing to do is to devise a compensation scheme. The services your potential employees will render should be duly compensated. It is imperative to research the salary ranges in your locality. For each position, set a salary range as the pay also depends on the worker's category. It is important to equate the salary with the qualifications and experience of those you intend to hire. Also, consider the inclusion of tips for specific jobs.

It is also important that you create an application form. Applicants should provide you with the information you need to know about them before you interview and hire them. Application forms enable you to get the information you need to properly evaluate applicants and a better comparison with other prospective employees. While resumes and application letters can provide more in-depth looks on applicants, they may lack the information you may need to decide whether to hire someone.

The application form can also serve as an agreement for applicants to deliver what they promised to deliver when you hire them. Application forms are generally signed for accuracy of the information, and you can use them to fire an employee that does not deliver as promised on the signed form. Completed application forms can also serve the purpose of verification to ensure that data from resumes are accurate and consistent.

The interview is about the most critical part of the hiring process, as it has the most significant weight for your final decision. It is important to note that the interview might not be very accurate in forecasting the actual ability of an employee as you might hope. Some applicants shine in interviews with their speaking skills and confidence but do not necessarily relate well with others or be loyal to you. Charm can influence you, so you should see through the veil of charm. To do this, ask questions that give you more objective information about the applicant. Ask about their interests and backgrounds. Ask for specific incidents that provide actual information about them. From the way they tell their experiences and interests, you may be able to see how they would relate with your customers and coworkers.

Though hypothetical questions may give you a glimpse as to how creative the applicant may be, they are not actual incidents that will accurately predict the applicant's behaviour. You should also ask to know what the applicant's expectations for the job are. This will show if the applicants understand the line of work well enough for you to consider employing them.

You should not decide to hire right away. Give yourself sometime after the interviews before offering the job to anyone. You must consider all applicants and evaluate all their qualities and skills to come up with a decision. You should come up with a shortlist of at least five people ranked according to your preference since you cannot expect everyone to take your offer immediately.

It is also important to hire good staff for your restaurant. With careful planning of job requirements and compensation system, with a careful selection of applicants, you are very close to having a successful restaurant.

CHAPTER EIGHT

Preparing a Business and Financial Plan

Most entrepreneurs of restaurant business get excited about the hustle and bustle of the kitchen. As a start-up restaurant entrepreneur, you must prepare yourself for the clashing and banging of pots and pans and the activities on the restaurant floor. Though preparing for the feats in a restaurant is not enough, many who attempted to start a restaurant business failed to do so because they overlooked an important aspect of the business, and that is the financial aspect. A lot of people fail to realise that a restaurant is a business that requires careful planning. Here is an outline of how preparing a business and financial plan is done.

A restaurant's business and financial plan is typically composed of eleven sections which cover the expected operations of a restaurant business under development.

1. Company Description

The business plan must begin with an overview of the entire profile of the restaurant under development. This section describes the business entity that will operate the restaurant. Details such as the company's founders, asset base, and type are stated in this section. Additional details are also stated, such as the company's Mission, Vision, corporate goals, the company's identity, and so on. The section would also describe the kind of restaurant being developed, its location, general target market and other information about the identity of the restaurant.

2. **Industry Analysis**

This section provides an overview of the restaurant industry. Careful research is needed for this section to provide accurate numbers regarding past trends and projected performance of the industry. This section explains why developing the restaurant is a worthwhile endeavour.

3. **Products and Services.**

This section describes the food and services the restaurant will offer. Here, the theme of the menu will be described. This section will also provide the general production scheme, stating how the food will be prepared and how other measures would be carried out in the production. The way upon which the service will be delivered will also be described here.

4. **Market Analysis.**

This section describes the target market segment. This should provide the profiles of the likely customers, as well as the locations where they will be coming from. The section will also include a description of the trends observed in the market, such as the population and other factors that might affect the restaurant's performance.

5. Competition

This section will describe the potential competitors' profiles and other restaurants within the area. Any restaurants within the same location that have the same target market will then be analysed further. The competitive strategy will then be described, stating how the new restaurant will be different from the existing ones.

6. Marketing Plans and Sales Strategies.

This section deals with the plan of action that would make the restaurant thrive. A description of how to penetrate the market will be given here. This section will also outline the channels that will be used for advertising and the generation of awareness about the restaurant. The budget allocated for the marketing strategy will also be specified here.

7. Operations.

This part of the plan will give the details of the operating scheme. It will describe the restaurant's equipment and facilities. The business hours of operation and the anticipated holidays will also be stated. Employee training, as well as other aspects of human resource management, will be described. The systems, controls, food production, and other services will be explained here.

8. Management and Organisation.

This section of the business plan will give the profiles of the Board, the Management team, as well as the ownership of the restaurant. The section will also describe the main employees and managers. Other information that will contain in this part of the document is the compensation and incentive scheme, management style and structure.

9. **Long-Term Development and Exit Plans.**

This section will provide the strategies, goals, and milestones of the restaurant. It will forecast the possibilities of expansion.

10. **Financial Data and Projections.**

This section will provide current information about the restaurant's assets at the beginning. It will also forecast sales, expenses, profits, taxes and so on.

11. **Appendices.**

This gives the actual data described in the main body of the business plan. The actual menu, financial statements, assets and other important information are stated here.

Having a restaurant does not only involve work in the kitchen or on the floor. A restaurant is a business, and the business aspect of its operations must also be emphasised.

CHAPTER NINE

Financing Your Restaurant Business

There are numerous problems involving money. Many individuals and businesses cater to those in need of financial assistance. Knowing when and where to borrow money or secure a loan for your business is crucial. Borrowing money, however, may be complicated especially with the pressure of the strict conditions set by the banks and other financial institutions involved in lending money. The most challenging part is to know when to borrow and from whom to borrow the money.

There are many reasons why an individual or a company may resort to borrowing money for their business, be it a start-up or an existing business. Some of the reasons include:

- To start their business
- For cash flow
- For business expansion

Therefore, the motivation behind the act of borrowing money differ; and people who have these common reasons for such loans have become targets for money lending institutions.

Below are the major sources of financial help:

- Banks
- Credit Unions
- Investors
- Family and Friends
- Others

THE DO'S OF BORROWING MONEY

1. **Research.**Before borrowing money from any source, be sure that the interest rate is reasonable.

2. **Compare.**Choose the borrower or financial institution that will give you the best value for your money.

3. **Consolidate.** By consolidating all you borrowing activities into one account, managing your finances will be a lot easier.

4. **Consider the contract.**Before you sign for a loan, make sure you will be able to abide with the rules set by the loan agreement.

5. Make sure you can pay the loan to avoid bad credit report.

6. **Borrow if it is a necessity.** Make sure that you really need the loan before you borrow, and that you are paying interest for a worthy endeavour.

7. Keep track of the deadline of repayments to avoid additional charges or fees.

Borrowing money may be frightening at first because of the risks involved. However, if you can invest the funds well and use it to earn more money to repay your debt, then it becomes a planned move with a lot of financial benefits. That is why the business plan, marketing analysis and other steps we have covered are critical.

FINDING INVESTORS

Financing your business may require you to obtain a loan. Otherwise, you may look for an investor to finance your business instead. Attracting investors can be done with the use of a good business plan, after which the problem will be on locating investors who would be willing to invest.

There are many ways to look for investors; the easiest of which is through your connections. Family members who are capable of investing are the people you can start presenting your business plan. Moreover, family friends, college friends or colleagues looking for ways to make money may be interested in your business venture.

Another method is to advertise. Finding investors with credible backgrounds is of paramount importance. These prospective investors are also on the lookout for promising business ideas, and they may be looking for something to invest on in classified ads where investment opportunities are advertised. Business owners have been able to locate investors this way. Just ensure that your investor will not end up stealing your business idea and start the business themselves.

Investors sometimes offer more than financial help in ensuring the success of a business. This is particularly true if your investor specialises in the same field or industry that your business is. These investors know the market very well and can give you sound advice on how to run your business. Also, as they spend their money in your business, they will be concerned about the status of the business and the return on their investment.

Borrowing money from a financial institution, or any investor for that matter, requires a high sense of responsibility. It is not something to belittle, and it should be accompanied with a good business plan to ensure repayment of the loan or the return on investment.

CHAPTER TEN

Choosing a Location for Your Restaurant

To set up a business involves the mastery of the four P's of marketing, namely: Product, Price, Place, and Promotion. Let us talk about the third P of the marketing mix, and that is looking for a suitable place (or location) for your restaurant business. A wrongly located business may mean the death of that business.

Before you choose a location for your restaurant business, you must be able to identify the following factors:

i. The kind of restaurant you want to establish
ii. Target market segment
iii. The budget set aside for rent or building cost
iv. Facilities needed to start up the business
v. The proximity of the business to your residence
vi. The amount of space needed to set-up the business
vii. Local laws relating to setting up your business

Evaluating the needs of the restaurant will help you find a suitable location that will allow you to attend to those needs. Without a clear representation of how the business is going to function and make a profit, making a wise and calculated decision on matters such as choosing a location will be very difficult.

SURVEYING THE POTENTIAL LOCATION OF THE BUSINESS

A thorough inspection of the neighbourhood or community surrounding the location where you plan to site your restaurant is important, to know if it is suitable for your business. Remember, your customers will be coming from the local community, so you must locate your business where you have many people who will patronise your food services.

Finding out whether the restaurant will thrive in a location is important in ensuring the success of your business. To do this, you need to take the following steps in surveying the neighbourhood:

1. **Do a physical survey of the location.**Spend time to survey the people in the area. Consider safety and cleanliness in your survey.

2. **Check out the competition.**Are there similar restaurant businesses established in the area? Find out.

3. **Get feedback from the community.**You may administer surveys in the place so you can analyse the behaviour of your target market. By so doing, you will have a good idea of how your restaurant will be accepted if it is situated in that area.

4. **Study the spending pattern of your target market.**It is wise to do a market survey of the area where you intend to locate your restaurant. (Refer to the chapter on Market Analysis for details).

5. **Foresee potential problems.**If you decide to site the restaurant in the said location, will there be any problems in the future?

6. **Determine space limitations and restrictions.**Determine whether available space meets your space requirements for your restaurant.

7. **Determine the anticipated costs**of setting up the restaurant in the chosen location. Factor in the costs of rent, equipment and labour.

8. **Analyse traffic flow and accessibility.**Is the location accessible by foot or using transportation? It is important to know how your prospective customers will access your location.

Depending on the type of your restaurant, the dynamics involving the decision to locate your business will also vary. Remember that what may work for a kind of business may not work for another. The reason is that not all businesses function the same way, and not all have the same target market. Therefore, these variations must be well-thought-out in making decisions regarding your restaurant business.

It is all about finding a perfect match between your business needs and what a location can offer your business. Finding a suitable place may not be easy, but it is necessary to ensure your business' success.